Thec

Prepare for your Theory T

Become a member with UK Driving Skills and get access to around 800+ Theory Test Revision Questions, produced under licence from the DVSA.

Hazard Perception

We also offer packages which allow you to study for the hazard perception test with access to over 130 official practise videos.

Visit us at www.ukdrivingskills.co.uk for more details.

ALSO FROM UK DRIVING SKILLS

Teaching a Learner Driver –
A guide for Amateur Instructors
Learning to Drive –
The Learner Driver's Manual
The Learner Driver's Logbook –
Lesson Plan & Progress Record
The Driving Test & How to Pass –
An Examiner's Guide to the 'L' Test

The Highway Code
How to Drive on a Motorway
Driving at Night & in Bad Weather

250 THEORY TEST QUESTIONS FOR:
Cars - Motorcycles - LGVs - PCVs

HIGHWAY CODE PLUS THEORY TEST QUESTIONS FOR:
Cars - Motorcycles - LGV - PCV - ADI

All available from www.ukdrivingskills.co.uk

THE LEARNER DRIVER'S LOGBOOK
DRIVING LESSON & PROGRESS RECORD

UK Driving Skills
Learning to Drive Series

Don L. Gates

www.ukdrivingskills.co.uk

Revised: 02/09/22

THE LEARNER DRIVER'S LOGBOOK

DRIVING LESSON
& PROGRESS RECORD

Contents

Introduction

Learning to drive is like picking up any new skill, it needs a planned and structured approach if it's to be successful. There's a lot to take in, a lot of rules to remember; and for most this can only be done one step at a time.

As your ability and experience develops, there comes a time when you must gain independence. You need to become a driver who is capable of making your own decisions and carrying them out safely. There's not much point in being constantly coached all the way through every lesson and then being abandoned to your own resources when you take a driving test. You must become largely independent before this time to know that you're ready for the test.

The transition from novice stage to test standard driving has to be brought about gradually; there are no clear cut borderlines between each level. This can only be accomplished by a skilled instructor who gets to know the capabilities of each student and keeps quiet when things are going along nicely, but is always ready to step in with a word of advice or encouragement when something out of the ordinary crops up or you appear uncertain of what to do.

Where does this process begin? At an early stage you'll begin to make simple decisions yourself such as when to change gear or give a signal. After repeated instruction on basic skills such as this, it should only be a short while before you anticipate the need for these actions yourself. You need not then be instructed in these areas apart from the occasional reminder.

This is how it works:

- The first stage of training is to be introduced to a new topic and to carry this out with help from your instructor.

- Stage two, is for you to carry out this new skill after being prompted by your instructor.

- At stage three, you should be acting by yourself in this area and only need occasional reminders.

- Stage four is reached when you can carry out the skill without the need of guidance or prompting.

It's only when you have reached stage four in all aspects of the driving test syllabus that you can claim you're ready for test. And you need to be able to demonstrate that you can do this consistently.

You can use the charts in this book to mark off and monitor your progress. Make sure that you and your instructor are both happy with each stage before ticking off the next level.

Included with each competence area are helpful tips and reminders, this will give you a handy reference to help you decide whether or not you have reached your goal in each area.

You'll not necessarily learn these topics in the order they are set out in this book; they are just laid out in logical groups.

There's also an area where you can write down your lesson appointment times; as well as the date and time of your driving test!

Eyesight

The first thing to assess before getting behind the wheel of a car is to make sure that your eyesight is up to standard; in fact it's a legal requirement.

You need to be able to read a vehicle number plate in good daylight from a minimum of 20m for new style plates, or 20.5m for older ones which have slightly larger symbols. If you pace this out you'll find that it's actually a very short distance. I would recommend that you're able to read the plate from well above this distance and to go for a proper eye examination if necessary.

If you normally need glasses or contact lenses to read a number plate, then you MUST wear these at all times when you're driving.

Controls

Precautions

Before starting the engine you should always make sure that the parking brake is applied and the gears are in neutral. If you start the engine in gear the car could suddenly drive forward out of control.

After a stall however, it's acceptable to hold the clutch down while re-starting. The parking brake should still be applied in this situation if the road is not level.

Accelerator

The accelerator needs to be used smoothly and at the right place and time. For instance, there's no point accelerating if you only need to brake again straight away.

You need to learn how to use 'deceleration', which is knowing when to take your foot 'off the gas' to control your speed instead of relying on the brakes.

Clutch

The clutch pedal should be operated smoothly without excessive jerkiness. You should be careful to avoid bringing the clutch up too high while waiting to move off which could cause the car to strain or pull forward.

Remember to put the clutch pedal down before stopping!

Gears

You need to know when to change gear, and to ensure that you're in the best gear for your speed and the road conditions. For example, trying to drive up a steep hill in a high gear could cause the car to labour or stall.

Avoid changing into low gears when you're travelling too fast, the 'engine braking' this causes can suddenly slow the car down and endanger anyone behind you.

Never 'coast' around corners or downhill with the clutch pedal down. This puts the car engine into neutral and can result in loss of control, particularly your speed (**Highway Code rule 122**). Although this refers to the clutch it's actually classed as a gear fault.

Always avoid looking down at the gear lever when making changes; you need to keep your eyes on the road.

Footbrake

Highway Code rules 114, 117 to 121

Braking should always be done in good time so that you avoid having to brake heavily. Light pressure at first, gradually increasing the pressure as you slow, and then relaxing the pressure at the end to avoid the 'bump' which happens if you leave too much pressure on the pedal.

You should avoid sudden braking except when this needs to be done in an emergency.

Parking Brake

You should apply the parking brake when stopping for more than a few seconds at a time, and always when the road is not level. It keeps the car secure and helps prevent you being pushed forward in the event of a rear collision.

Even in an automatic car you should still use the parking brake. Although you may not roll back, the car will have a tendency to creep forward. If you rely only on the footbrake to prevent this, your brake lights will dazzle the driver behind at night and in poor conditions (**Highway Code rule 114**).

Steering

The recommended way to steer is the 'push pull' method, keeping your hands on either side of the wheel means that you have instant ability to change direction either way. Also in modern cars, there's usually an airbag in the centre of the steering wheel, if you're crossing your hands at a time when this went off it could lead to serious injury rather than protecting you.

It's acceptable to cross your hands when manoeuvring at low speeds, such as when doing a parking exercise.

Operation of the wheel should be smooth and steady, avoiding sudden or late movements. You need to plan a course which takes you clear of any obstructions in good time.

Avoid letting go of the wheel; allowing it to spin freely means that you're not fully in control and you could be thrown off course if you hit a bump or pothole.

Ancillary Controls

These include things such as lights, horn, windscreen washers and wipers, demisters etc. You should know where all of these are and be capable of operating them confidently whilst driving along. These will be tested as part of the 'show me tell me' questions when you take a driving test. Make sure that you practice using all these controls on a regular basis, even if they're not required at the time you're driving. You can find a copy of these in the annex at the back of the book.

Controls				
	New topic under instruction	Carried out when prompted	Rarely needs prompting	No prompting required
Precautions				
Accelerator				
Clutch				
Gears				
Footbrake				
Parking brake				
Steering				
Ancillary controls				

Controls

Notes

Moving Off

Highway Code rules 159, 211

Safety

Observation needs to be taken all around your car using interior and exterior mirrors, and a blind spot check should be taken just before you set off. If you stall or there's some other delay, look again!

Give a signal if it will help people, but think before you put this on. For example, if you signal just as someone is about to pass you they may think you're about to set off right away. This can distract or even intimidate another road user (particularly on two wheels). The only time you should sit with a signal showing is if the traffic is heavy and the only way you can move off is if someone has to slow or stop to let you out.

Make sure before you go that you have judged not only the size of gap but also the speed of any approaching traffic. You must not cause anyone to change speed or direction.

If you're moving off at an angle (around a parked car or other obstruction), make sure that you also pay attention to any oncoming traffic that may be affected.

Control

When moving off either on a gradient or on the level, the technique is basically the same. The clutch should be brought up to the biting point with just enough 'gas' to enable you to pull away safely. On a gradient you'll need to accelerate more firmly and look for a bigger gap (hill start).

You need to aim for a smooth engagement of the clutch to avoid any jerkiness, and ensure that you're in the correct gear. If the clutch is used correctly you should not roll back.

If you stall, make sure that you go through the 'precautions' procedure and that you're in the correct gear to get going again. Stalling is not a problem providing that you regain control safely and don't spend too long moving off.

Cars with diesel engines have more pulling power at low speeds and don't stall so easily, but your technique for moving off should be no different to that used in a petrol engine car.

Move away smoothly without excessive acceleration, and ensure that you steer safely around any obstruction (angle start) and into your normal driving position.

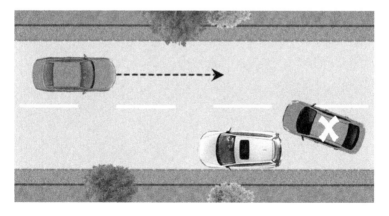

On the angle start, the car marked with an X should
not pull out until the oncoming driver has passed

Moving off

	New topic under instruction	Carried out when prompted	Rarely needs prompting	No prompting required
Safely				
Control (level)				
Hill start				
Angle start				

Notes

Moving off

Notes

Use of Mirrors

Highway Code rules 97, 133, 159, 161, 163, 179, 180, 182, 211, 202, 229, 239

Before signalling

It's important to know what may be behind you before you signal your intention to turn. You need to know if what you're about to do will affect anyone, and if someone is particularly close then you will be able to signal earlier to give them more warning.

Changing direction

This is one of the most important skills, and an area which leads to many driving test failures. It's vitally important that a driver is always aware of what is behind and to the sides before changing direction. Always use your mirrors before doing so.

But just looking is not enough; you must look early enough, judge what may happen, and act safely on what you see.

Use your mirrors well before you need to change direction, consider whether a signal is required, and make sure that any other road user is aware of your intentions before you move. You must be careful not to cause anyone else to alter speed or direction when changing lanes.

Changing speed

You also need to be aware of what may be behind you before using your brakes, particularly when approaching hazards such as traffic lights. You may need to reduce speed in case you have to stop if the lights change. Knowing what is behind you and how close they are will influence your decision making here.

If you intend to pull in to stop or park somewhere, again use your mirrors well before so that you're aware of any following traffic. Signal if necessary to warn others before you start to brake and move over.

Use of Mirrors

	New topic under instruction	Carried out when prompted	Rarely needs prompting	No prompting required
Before signalling				
Changing direction				
Changing speed				

Notes

Use of Mirrors

Notes

Giving Signals

Highway Code rule 103

Where necessary

Other road users need to be kept informed of your intentions so that they have time to react if they are going to be affected in any way. You don't need to signal if there's no-one who will be affected, but don't overlook pedestrians who may be about to cross the road!

Correctly

Ensure that your signals are not going to be misleading. For instance, by giving an unnecessary signal as you gradually move out to pass a parked car - if there's a junction opposite; people may think you're turning. Never wave others on at junctions.

Signalling too early can be misleading if it's left on for too long. Particularly if you pass areas which others may think you're pulling into, or if you pass junctions before the one you intend to take.

Always ensure that signals are cancelled after you have turned or changed lanes. Leaving them on is a very common error.

Properly timed

For the purposes of the driving test, this relates to signals that are given too late to be of any value (signals given too early are assessed under 'correct' use.) Don't leave others guessing, particularly in a situation where they might get stuck behind you, such as when you're turning right.

17

Giving Signals

	New topic under instruction	Carried out when prompted	Rarely needs prompting	No prompting required
Where necessary				
Correctly				
Properly timed				

Notes

Junctions

Highway Code rules 170 to 190, rule 211

Approach speed

The speed at which you should approach a junction depends on the view you have available, and the amount of traffic going through it. You should always approach at a speed that gives you time to look properly, and allows you to stop comfortably if you need to give way. The more restricted the view, the slower the approach speed needs to be.

Observation

Effective observation is not just about looking in a particular direction; it's about judgement. If you have approached at the proper speed, then you should have plenty of time to look. Irrelevant of which direction you're going in, you need to take effective observation in all directions, not only to spot approaching traffic, but also potential obstructions or pedestrians in your path.

Judgement means knowing when it's safe to emerge without causing others to take action to avoid you. You need to judge the speed and distance of any approaching traffic, and make sure that you have time to pull out and accelerate safely away.

Turning right

When turning right you need to ensure that you get into the appropriate position in good time; but not so early that you impede other traffic. The busier the road is however, the sooner you will need to make your move.

Be guided by any road markings which will guide you into the correct lane, sometimes there may be more than one lane available.

Be aware of the type of road that you're on. A dual-carriageway or multi-lane road will mean a change of lanes. In a one-way street you need to go over to the right hand side of the road as soon as it's safe to do so.

If you're turning right at a yellow box junction, ensure you go forward into it provided your exit is not blocked by anything other than oncoming traffic.

Cutting corners

When turning right into a side road you should avoid turning too early and 'cutting the corner' of the road you're turning into (driving over the centre line). To do this when the road is narrow or the view ahead is restricted can be dangerous.

Turning left

Don't approach a left turn so close to the kerb that you end up making contact with it, but nor should you be too wide. In particular you must avoid swinging out to the right before turning.

Where there's a slip lane available to filter off to the left, ensure you move into this straight away, especially if there's traffic behind which could otherwise come up on your inside and cut you off.

Junctions

	New topic under instruction	Carried out when prompted	Rarely needs prompting	No prompting required
Approach speed				
Observation				
Turning left				
Turning right				
Cutting corners				

Notes

Junctions

Notes

Judgement

Overtaking

Highway Code rules 129, 162 to 169, 191, 212 to 213, 215

If you need to overtake a slower moving vehicle, particularly a cyclist or horse rider, it's vital that you give them plenty of room as you pass. This is even more important in windy weather when a cyclist is likely to be blown off course.

Don't leave it until the last moment to pull out, and ensure that you have enough time and space to pass without encountering any oncoming traffic. Once you have overtaken don't cut back in too soon.

You should never overtake where your view of the road ahead is restricted, or on the approach to a junction.

There are some places where you MUST not overtake:

- if you would have to cross double white lines with a solid line nearest to you (except to pass an obstruction)
- if you would have to enter an area of chevrons if it's surrounded by a solid white line
- within the zigzag lines on the approach to a crossing
- if you would have to enter a bus, tram or cycle lane during its times of operation
- where there's a 'no overtaking' sign

Meeting

When you have to pull out to pass an obstruction with traffic coming towards you, this is described as 'meeting'. Don't go through a gap unless you're sure you can do so without forcing others to brake or pull aside.

Speed and clearance are also issues here. You need to make sure you have adequate clearance on both side of your car, and if the space is limited then keep your speed low.

Don't be tempted to play 'follow the leader'. Just because one or two cars ahead of you go through a gap, don't make the mistake of thinking that it's okay to follow them. Make sure you can also get through without encountering oncoming traffic.

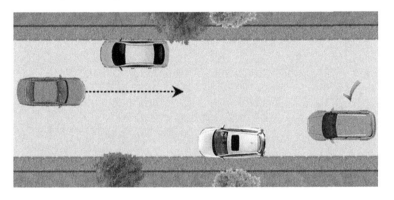

The driver on the right is holding back to wait for the oncoming car

Crossing

When turning right across the path of oncoming traffic, it's important that you don't obstruct anyone's progress, or cause them to veer around you. Faults in this area can often be dangerous and you should always wait when you're in doubt.

24

Judgement

	New topic under instruction	Carried out when prompted	Rarely needs prompting	No prompting required
Overtaking				
Meeting				
Crossing				

Notes

Judgement

Notes

Positioning

Normal driving

Highway Code rule 160

Your normal position should be on the left except when signs or road markings tell you otherwise. Be aware of any bus lanes, sometimes they only operate at peak traffic times and the rest of the day they can and should be used as your normal lane.

Avoid driving too far out from the kerb, particularly when then there's traffic coming towards you; but you should not drive so close to the kerb that you're bouncing in and out of the sinks!

Lane discipline

Highway Code rules 133 to 142, 184 to 186

When you have two or more lanes, you should avoid straddling these wherever possible. If you need to pass an obstruction or two, there's no problem with straddling lanes for a short distance while you do this. Where there are regular obstructions however, you should change lanes until you're safely past them all.

You need to plan ahead and make sure that you choose the appropriate lane in good time so as to avoid unnecessary changes.

When going through junctions, roundabouts in particular you should ensure that you don't needlessly cross from one lane to another.

27

Normal stops

Highway Code rules 156, 191, 238 to 252, 291, 302

When choosing a position to make a 'normal stop' or park, you need to ask yourself two questions; is it safe, and is it legal?

Stop close to the kerb, and in a position where you'll not obstruct others, or block someone's view; for instance by parking close to a junction. Wherever possible avoid stopping opposite other vehicles where this will make the road narrower.

Here are other examples of where you should not park:

- near a school entrance
- where you would prevent access for emergency vehicles
- at or near a bus / tram stop or taxi rank
- on the approach to a level crossing
- near the brow of a hill, hump bridge or a bend
- opposite a traffic island
- where the kerb has been lowered

Positioning

	New topic under instruction	Carried out when prompted	Rarely needs prompting	No prompting required
Normal driving				
Lane discipline				
Normal stops				

Notes

Positioning

Notes

Awareness

Pedestrian crossings

Highway Code rule 191 to 199

Whatever type of pedestrian crossing you approach it should always be at the correct speed. You need to anticipate where lights may change or if someone might step up to a zebra crossing and ensure that you react safely and in good time.

You should always be prepared to stop when someone is waiting at a zebra crossing, but you MUST stop if anyone places a foot onto the road.

Don't wave anyone onto a crossing; they may step out without looking into the path of another vehicle.

In queuing traffic don't block a crossing by stopping on it.

At a pelican crossing, give way to anyone still on the crossing when the amber light flashes; otherwise be ready to move on when it's safe.

Planning

Highway Code rules 146, 147, 170

This is something that improves with experience, but you always need to look as far ahead as you can and anticipate what is going to happen before you get there.

You need to think not only about your own actions, but to predict the actions of those around you. Look for clues in the way that other people position or change their speed, can you see where they are looking and what do you think they might be about to do? Things happening on the road, or about to come onto the road, should not take you by surprise if you're showing proper anticipation and planning.

Also, be prepared to give way to pedestrians who are crossing or waiting to cross a road which you are turning into.

Clearance

When passing parked cars and other obstructions you should always give them adequate clearance wherever possible. As a rule, you should not get any closer to a stationary car than an open door's width. There are times when this may not be possible however, in which case you need to reduce speed and check to make sure that no-one is about to open their door.

Following distance

Highway Code rules 126, 227, 230, 235, 260

When following another vehicle it's important to maintain a safe distance in case they suddenly need to stop.

Keeping well back will also enable you to see further ahead as well as giving you more time to react. The larger the vehicle, the more it will block your view, so the further back you need to be from it.

As a guideline, you should maintain at least a two second gap ahead. This distance should be increased in bad weather as your stopping distance can be much greater when the roads are wet or icy. This also applies to night-time or other poor conditions where your visibility will be reduced.

Awareness

	New topic under instruction	Carried out when prompted	Rarely needs prompting	No prompting required
Pedestrian crossings				
Planning				
Clearance				
Following distance				

Notes

Awareness

Notes

Progress

Use of speed

Highway Code 124 to 126, 146, 152 to 154, 205 to 209, 214

It should go without saying that you need to obey speed limits, but it's not just a question of what the speed limit is; but whether your speed is suitable for the conditions and the area you're driving in.

If you enter a sharp bend too fast or hit a speed hump and lose control of your car for instance, this would not be acceptable. Driving on narrow and busy roads without slowing down when necessary would not be considered safe, particularly if there are pedestrians and children at risk. The busier the road, the slower your speed needs to be to give you time to see and react to hazards.

The basic rule of advice is that you should always be able to stop comfortably within the distance you can see to be clear. If you find that you're having to brake heavily in response to hazards, then you're probably driving too fast.

Normal progress

This differs from 'use of speed', in that it relates to making adequate progress whenever it's safe to do so.

A good driver should always be aware of the speed limit for the road they are driving on, and although it may not necessarily always be safe to drive at that limit, you should not drive so slowly that you're holding up and frustrating other drivers.

You also need to vary your rate of acceleration depending on the type of road you're on. Building up speed slowly is fine on a busy shopping street, but on an open main road you should be ready to pull away and reach a reasonable speed without undue delay where safety and conditions permit.

Undue hesitation

In your early stages of driving it's natural that you may be overcautious, particularly when it comes to emerging at junctions. There's a difference however between when you *could* go and when you *should* go. You need to develop confidence and judgement so that you can make safe decisions without 'undue' delay. If you loiter without reason when there's an obvious opportunity to move on you may eventually find people sounding their horns in frustration or they may even start to come around you.

Progress

	New topic under instruction	Carried out when prompted	Rarely needs prompting	No prompting required
Use of speed				
Normal progress				
Undue hesitation				

Notes

Progress

Notes

Signs & Signals

Traffic signs

Highway Code rules 109, 142, 184

You need to be able to recognise and respond to traffic signs in good time. These include signs informing you of a change in speed limit, direction arrows on traffic islands, no-entry and stop signs, and also signs which inform you about lane usage.

Looking well ahead will enable you to spot signs earlier, and give you a chance to react safely before reaching them. You'll find them on posts at either side of the road, and at larger busier junctions, they may also be seen on overhead gantries.

Having a good knowledge of what those signs means is essential for safe and legal driving, as signs are often mandatory and must be obeyed.

Road markings

Highway Code rules 127 to 131, 140 to 141, 174, 185, 238, 247

Similarly with traffic signs, you need to recognise the meaning of road markings and respond in good time to them.

As they are on the road surface as opposed to sign posts, they are not so easy to spot, and can be difficult to read when in wet conditions, especially when the sun is out after rain.

You may also find that traffic ahead of you will hide those markings, which is another reason for keeping your distance when following other vehicles; it will give you more chance to 'read the road.'

Lane markings may sometimes be used just to guide you, for instance by indicating which lane you need for a particular destination, but where there are lane arrows you must ensure that you follow them.

White chevrons or hatched markings will be found where traffic needs to be separated; where these have a broken border you may enter them if necessary (though not without a valid reason), but you MUST not enter an area with a solid border except in an emergency.

When you're in queuing traffic, be on the lookout for 'keep clear' markings and ensure you don't block anyone's access.

Yellow box junctions are often misunderstood, make sure you know the rules as set out in the **Highway Code rule 174**.

Traffic lights

Highway Code rules 175 to 178, 293

It should go without saying that you need to know what traffic light signals mean, but it's surprising how many people either don't know the rules or choose to ignore them. Because of this, never assume that it's always safe to go when you get the green light. Always look the way you would at any other junction to make that it's safe to proceed.

Approach traffic lights the way you would any other hazard, anticipate that they may change and adjust your speed accordingly. For instance, a light that has been green for a long time may well be about to change, and similarly if a green filter light is on, they generally don't last for very long. Use your mirrors, slow down, and be ready to stop.

You should never have to brake heavily at lights, this is often the cause of rear-end collisions. There are times when it may be safer to go through an amber light rather than stop at it, but if are approaching at an appropriate speed you'll have more time to make your decision.

Traffic controllers

Highway Code rules 105 to 108, 210

You may sometime encounter people who are controlling traffic, either as a routine such as a school crossing patrol, or in the event of a traffic light failure where the police or a traffic warden may step in. At roadworks you may find someone controlling traffic flow with 'stop / go' boards. These are all traffic controllers, and they MUST be obeyed.

Be particularly aware of school crossing patrols; they don't have to step into the road in order to stop you, it's enough for them to display their sign at the kerbside.

Other road users

Highway Code rules 104, 219

When another road user gives a signal, you need to be aware of what they are about to do, and ensure that you respond in good time. Particular situations that will need you to react may be when the driver ahead of you signals their intention to stop, or indicates a right turn. You should be ready to change position if necessary to avoid them.

Be aware of buses that have stopped, if they signal to move out again, you should allow them to do so if it's safe.

Emergency vehicles also come into this area. If you hear sirens or see flashing blue lights, always be ready to stop or move out of their way but be careful not to over-react. Suddenly braking or changing direction may endanger others, so you must act early enough to ensure that whatever you do is safe. There's no point avoiding an ambulance if you suddenly swerve into the path of a cyclist!

Signs & Signals

	New topic under instruction	Carried out when prompted	Rarely needs prompting	No prompting required
Traffic signs				
Road markings				
Traffic lights				
Traffic controllers				
Other road users				

Notes

Signs & Signals

Notes

The Exercises

Emergency stop

Highway Code rules 118 to 120

Most modern cars are now equipped with anti-lock braking systems, so the likelihood of skidding is much reduced. It's still important however, that you know how to stop your car as quickly as possible should the need arise. I would not recommend doing this on every lesson, but occasional practise is needed.

You need to ensure that you're on a quiet road where there's no traffic behind you, your instructor or accompanying driver should make sure of this.

The two important parts of this exercise are the speed of your reactions, and the effectiveness of your braking. When you're signalled to stop, you need to react instantly, and brake firmly but without excessive force.

In the event of a skid, you need to know what to do to regain control, and ensure that you can do this without panicking.

Reversing

Highway Code rules 200 to 203

Reversing around a corner is no longer an exercise that you'll be asked to do on a driving test, but it's still a skill that you need to learn. There will be occasions where you need to reverse into a road in order to turn your car around.

45

You should practise in an area where you'll not get in the way of other traffic. The aim of this exercise is for you to reverse around the corner with reasonable accuracy, neither making contact with the kerb, nor drifting too far away from it. You need to maintain a steady course, and ensure that you don't drift so wide that you'll make it difficult for anything coming up behind to get past you.

All round observation is vital if this is to be done safely. Check all around your car before you begin, and keep checking all the way through the reverse. Check to the front and side before your bonnet starts to swing out. Although it's acceptable to use your left hand door mirror to help with accuracy, you MUST not be tempted to stare in it and neglect proper observation to the rear and all around the vehicle.

Should any other road users approach while you're reversing, always be ready to stop and let them pass, or if necessary, pull forward to let them out of the junction.

Pulling up on the right

Highway Code rule 239 tells us 'do not park facing against the traffic flow', yet for some reason the Driving Standards Agency decided to introduce this exercise into the driving test.

There are two elements to the exercise, the first being to pull up in a safe place on the right. Consider the advice given for making a 'normal stop' and put that into practise.

The additional problem here is that you may have to contend with oncoming traffic before crossing over. After checking to see what is behind you, choose your safe stopping place and if needed, signal your intention to go to the right. If there's oncoming traffic, simply treat this as though you were turning into a side road... slow down, stop if necessary and wait for a safe gap before pulling over.

Once in position, you'll be asked to reverse in a straight line for a couple of car lengths keeping reasonably close to the kerb. This should be a simple exercise though you do need to ensure that you take proper observation. Consider that you may be reversing across driveways, and any pedestrians nearby may possibly want to cross the road, so check over you right hand shoulder as well as to the front and rear before you set off. The bulk of your observation should be over your left hand shoulder while reversing with regular checks to the front and right. If vehicles approach from the rear, you may be able to continue going back without affecting them depending on how wide the road is, though anything coming from the front has to move out to go around you, so you'll almost certainly need to pause while they do this.

Having completed the reverse you'll then be asked to move off when you're ready. Again, all round checks should be taken, finishing with a good look ahead and a blind-spot check over your left shoulder to make sure you can pull away and back to your normal driving position without affecting anything coming from the front or rear.

Parallel parking

This is something you need to do when reversing into a space between cars on the road, although for the purposes of practise and the driving test, you may reverse around a car without having another one behind you.

As you move into your starting position, be careful not to obstruct any other vehicles. Signal in good time and slow down next to the gap you're going to back into to show people what you're going to do; then adjust your position if necessary before you begin.

Get into reverse gear quickly so that your reversing lights will warn anyone approaching from behind what you intend to do. If you're lucky anyone coming from behind may then go around you and continue on their way. Sometimes they will stay behind but don't be tempted to wave them past; you could bring them into conflict with another road user. Check all around and when it's safe, begin to reverse at a slow steady pace, remembering to check that your bonnet doesn't swing into the path of any oncoming vehicles.

- A - turn the wheel quickly towards the kerb
- B - straighten up the wheel
- C - turn the wheel quickly away from the kerb
- D - straighten up the wheel & pull forward if necessary to tidy up

If you're reversing around a single car, you should aim to complete the exercise within about two car lengths. Don't go back too far.

If you think you're about to hit the kerb or are too far out, stop and pull forward a little to correct the error, though do be careful to look round before changing position to ensure you don't get in anyone's way. It's okay to adjust your position but try to make as few moves as you can.

You need to finish parallel to, and reasonably close to the kerb.

Reverse into a bay

Most of the advice given for parallel parking should be followed here with regards to control and observation, although the objective is of course different. The aim is to reverse into a bay and finish with your car between the lines.

The easiest way to carry out this manoeuvre, is to pull up alongside the bay you want to reverse into, then after making sure it's safe, move slowly forward and steer sharply away from the bay, so that the back of your car begins to line up with the bay behind you, then straighten up your wheels before stopping so that you're ready to reverse on as straight a course as possible into the bay, adjusting the steering as you go.

If there are bays opposite the one you're reversing into, you can make things easier for yourself by driving forwards partly into a bay on the opposite side, and then reversing straight into the bay behind you. Make sure that the bays are lined up opposite each other before doing this however as they may sometimes be staggered!

You need to avoid finishing on, or too close to the white lines, as this could make it difficult for anyone parking next to you to open their doors.

Forward parking into bay

The **Highway Code rule 201** states 'Do not reverse from a side road into a main road. When using a driveway, reverse in and drive out if you can.' But here we have another DVSA exercise which contravenes that advice, as it asks you to drive forward into a bay and then reverse out of it!

Aim for a bay which is in a clear space if possible, as attempting to drive into one where your space is restricted by other vehicles will make the job much more difficult.

In this situation, the fact that you're going to pull into a bay should be pretty obvious, so you're unlikely to take anyone by surprise by doing this, but it doesn't take away the need to keep a check all around your car both when taking up your starting position and while doing the exercise. If you're a little on the slow side, there's always the risk that someone else may try to come past you.

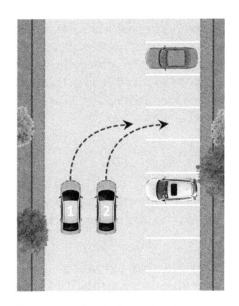

Position approaching the forward parking exercise –
Car 1 is in a much better position than car 2

Aim to finish with all your wheels between one set of bay markings, it doesn't matter if you cross the lines while doing the exercise, it's your finish position which counts. But two things to avoid are overshooting into another bay in front, or taking too many shunts.

Once you're finished within the bay, you'll need to reverse out to the right or the left; be aware that some car parks may have one-way systems in operation!

Be careful to keep an eye on your bonnet, if you steer too soon you may be in danger if getting too close to anything parked next to you. You don't need to reverse out in a straight line however, if there's room you may steer right away, it does not matter if you cross the lines while backing out.

This is the point when you're quite likely to come into conflict with drivers and pedestrians. Ensure that you check all around before you reverse and keep the observation going until you're safely out. Be prepared to stop if anyone is approaching who may be affected, and then continue again as soon as it's safe after making further checks.

Turn in the road (Three point turn)

This is another exercise which was dropped from the driving test, but is still an important one to learn. If you inadvertently turn into a cul-de-sac, this may be the only way you can turn around.

The object of the exercise is to turn you car to face the opposite way, keeping within the road; you should avoid touching the kerbs or entering people's driveways etc.

It's an exercise in control; you should use the clutch and parking brake to prevent your car from rolling backwards or forwards during the exercise.

It does not have to be completed in three shunts, but your steering should be used efficiently to make the least number of moves.

Observation is also important, checking all around before you start the exercise to make sure that you don't obstruct anyone; and once you have started, keep the observation going. You may have to carry on once you have started, as you will be partly blocking the road, but in particular look out for cyclists who may try to sneak past and be ready to wait for them.

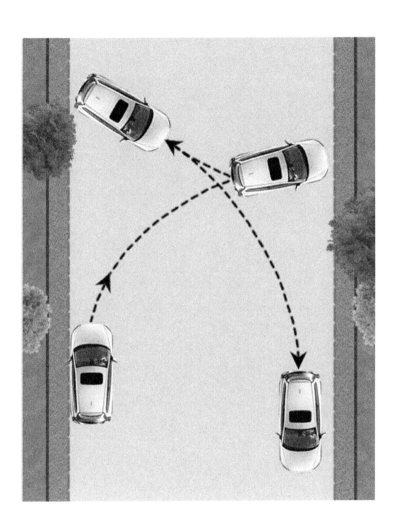

Exercises

	New topic under instruction	Carried out when prompted	Rarely needs prompting	No prompting required
Emergency stop				
Reversing				
Pulling up on right				
Parallel parking				
Reverse into a bay				
Forward parking				
Turn in the road				

Notes

Exercises

Notes

Exercises

Notes

Appointments

Date & Time	Location	Comments

Appointments		
Date & Time	Location	Comments

Appointments

Date & Time	Location	Comments

Appointments

Date & Time	Location	Comments

Appointments		
Date & Time	Location	Comments

Appointments		
Date & Time	Location	Comments

Appointments		
Date & Time	Location	Comments

Appointments		
Date & Time	Location	Comments

Show Me Tell Me Questions

1. About the questions

You'll be asked two vehicle safety questions during your driving test.

The examiner will ask you one:

- 'tell me' question (where you explain how you'd carry out a safety task) at the start of your test, before you start driving
- 'show me' question (where you show how you'd carry out a safety task) while you're driving

You'll get one driving fault (sometimes called a 'minor') if you get one or both questions wrong.

You will fail your test if your driving is dangerous or potentially dangerous while you answer the 'show me' question.

2. 'Tell me' questions

1. Tell me how you'd check that the brakes are working before starting a journey.

Brakes should not feel spongy or slack. Brakes should be tested as you set off. Vehicle should not pull to one side.

2. Tell me where you'd find the information for the recommended tyre pressures for this car and how tyre pressures should be checked.

Manufacturer's guide, use a reliable pressure gauge, check and adjust pressures when tyres are cold, don't forget spare tyre, remember to refit valve caps.

3. Tell me how you make sure your head restraint is correctly adjusted so it provides the best protection in the event of a crash.

The head restraint should be adjusted so the rigid part of the head restraint is at least as high as the eye or top of the ears, and as close to the back of the head as is comfortable. Note: Some restraints might not be adjustable.

4. Tell me how you'd check the tyres to ensure that they have sufficient tread depth and that their general condition is safe to use on the road.

No cuts and bulges, 1.6mm of tread depth across the central three-quarters of the breadth of the tyre, and around the entire outer circumference of the tyre.

5. Tell me how you'd check that the headlights and tail lights are working. You don't need to exit the vehicle.

Explain you'd operate the switch (turn on ignition if necessary), then walk round vehicle (as this is a 'tell me' question, you don't need to physically check the lights).

6. Tell me how you'd know if there was a problem with your anti-lock braking system.

Warning light should illuminate if there is a fault with the anti-lock braking system.

7. Tell me how you'd check the direction indicators are working. You don't need to exit the vehicle.

Explain you'd operate the switch (turn on ignition if necessary), and then walk round vehicle (as this is a 'tell me' question, you don't need to physically check the lights).

8. Tell me how you'd check the brake lights are working on this car.

Explain you'd operate the brake pedal, make use of reflections in windows or doors, or ask someone to help.

9. Tell me how you'd check the power-assisted steering is working before starting a journey.

If the steering becomes heavy, the system may not be working properly. Before starting a journey, 2 simple checks can be made.

Gentle pressure on the steering wheel, maintained while the engine is started, should result in a slight but noticeable movement as the system begins to operate. Alternatively turning the steering wheel just after moving off will give an immediate indication that the power assistance is functioning.

10. Tell me how you'd switch on the rear fog light(s) and explain when you'd use it/them. You don't need to exit the vehicle.

Operate switch (turn on dipped headlights and ignition if necessary). Check warning light is on. Explain use.

11. Tell me how you switch your headlight from dipped to main beam and explain how you'd know the main beam is on.

Operate switch (with ignition or engine on if necessary), check with main beam warning light.

12. Open the bonnet and tell me how you'd check that the engine has sufficient oil.

Identify dipstick/oil level indicator, describe check of oil level against the minimum and maximum markers.

13. Open the bonnet and tell me how you'd check that the engine has sufficient engine coolant.

Identify high and low level markings on header tank where fitted or radiator filler cap, and describe how to top up to correct level.

14. Open the bonnet and tell me how you'd check that you have a safe level of hydraulic brake fluid.

Identify reservoir, check level against high and low markings.

You need to open the bonnet and tell the examiner how you'd do the check if you're asked question 12, 13 or 14.

3. 'Show me' questions

When it's safe to do so, can you show me how you wash and clean the rear windscreen?

When it's safe to do so, can you show me how you wash and clean the front windscreen?

When it's safe to do so, can you show me how you'd switch on your dipped headlights?

When it's safe to do so, can you show me how you'd set the rear demister?

When it's safe to do so, can you show me how you'd operate the horn?

When it's safe to do so, can you show me how you'd demist the front windscreen?

When it's safe to do so, can you show me how you'd open and close the side window?

The Learning to Drive Series

The Highway Code &
Theory Test Revision Questions

Teaching a Learner Driver
(A Guide for Amateur Instructors)

Learning to Drive
(The Learner Driver's Manual)

The Learner Driver's Logbook
(Lesson Plan & Progress Record)

The Driving Test
(An Examiner's Guide to the L Test)

Everything you need to prepare
for driving test success and a
lifetime of safe driving!

71

.

Printed in Great Britain
by Amazon

87686682R00047